POSTMODERN ENCOUNTERS

Plato and
the Internet

Kieron O'Hara

Series editor: Richard Appignanesi

ICON BOOKS UK

TOTEM BOOKS USA

Published in the UK in 2002
by Icon Books Ltd., Grange Road,
Duxford, Cambridge CB2 4QF
E-mail: info@iconbooks.co.uk
www.iconbooks.co.uk

Published in the USA in 2002
by Totem Books
Inquiries to: Icon Books Ltd.,
Grange Road, Duxford,
Cambridge CB2 4QF, UK

Sold in the UK, Europe, South Africa
and Asia by Faber and Faber Ltd.,
3 Queen Square, London WC1N 3AU
or their agents

Distributed to the trade in the USA by
National Book Network Inc.,
4720 Boston Way, Lanham,
Maryland 20706

Distributed in the UK, Europe,
South Africa and Asia by
Macmillan Distribution Ltd.,
Houndmills, Basingstoke RG21 6XS

Distributed in Canada by
Penguin Books Canada,
10 Alcorn Avenue, Suite 300,
Toronto, Ontario M4V 3B2

Published in Australia in 2002
by Allen & Unwin Pty. Ltd.,
83 Alexander Street,
Crows Nest, NSW 2065

Text copyright © 2002 Kieron O'Hara

The author has asserted his moral rights.

Series editor: Richard Appignanesi

ISBN 1 84046 346 5

Typesetting by Wayzgoose

Printed and bound in the UK by
Cox & Wyman Ltd., Reading

The Knowledge Economy

We are now living, we are often told, in a knowledge economy. In the past, the key to wealth was a plentiful supply of labour and control of natural resources. Nowadays, though, developments in technology – particularly computer and telecommunications technology – have resulted in undreamt-of ease in transferring data around the world. A scientific paper written yesterday in New York can be running off the printers today in researchers' offices in San Francisco, London, Sydney, Tokyo or Beijing. Scientists can collaborate without ever meeting face to face. Desktop computers can alert their operators to the latest news items, stock prices or cricket scores as they change.

In this new world, the important source of competitive advantage for a developed economy is no longer raw materials or labour, but *knowledge*: bright ideas, smart designs, clever organisation. It can't compete in brawn, so it must use brain. The new economy demands *knowledge workers* who create value and wealth, not with traditional money capital, but with *intellectual capital*.[1] Indeed, many hold out the hope that the exploitation of knowledge could be a key to enriching the developing world too, in that knowledge capital is easier to find and cheaper to get hold of than money capital, and the World Bank's Global Development Network has been set up to explore that possibility.[2]

All this is independent of the dotcom boom and bust. Knowledge is big business in any industry. A huge amount is invested annually in knowledge via research and development programmes, staff training, and so on; but because knowledge is intangible, it can't be measured or accounted for. As consultant Alan Burton-Jones puts it, 'knowledge is transforming the nature of production and thus work, jobs, the firm, the market, and every aspect of economic activity. Yet knowledge is currently a poorly understood and thus undervalued economic resource.'[3]

What is Knowledge? The Discipline of Epistemology

So it makes sense, in this new world, to get to know about knowledge itself: what it is, how you spot it, how you make sure you have enough of it. It turns out that there are people who investigate these issues – the study of knowledge is a branch of philosophy called *epistemology*. Epistemologists investigate such questions as: What is knowledge? Are there different types of knowledge? Are there procedures that you can follow to make sure you acquire knowledge? How do you know that something *is* knowledge? How do you discover whether you are mistaken? Can you know what you don't know?

Epistemology is not the oldest branch of philosophy, but damn near. The first philosopher whose epistemological work has come down to us in any quantity is Plato (*c.* 428–*c.* 347 BC). Such was the power of his influence on later philosophers that much epistemology since has continued along more or less the same lines. Indeed, even in the present day, epistemologists are wrestling with problems (and providing answers) that bear a strong resemblance to Plato's.

In this twenty-first-century context, there are many dilemmas that Plato would recognise. For instance, how do we sort out the knowledge from the dross on the World Wide Web, the true from the false? Even so, can it be right that epistemology should still operate from essentially Ancient Greek assumptions? Does the emergence of massive and thoroughgoing technological change make *no* difference to the epistemological landscape? Or alternatively, do we need to look afresh at the phenomenon of knowledge in the Internet age?

This is the question I will examine in this book. I will sketch the traditional philosophical arguments, to give a rough idea of the general Platonic position that still holds sway today. Then I'll talk about the technological, commercial and political context which has made the study of knowledge suddenly so pressing. To close, I'll bring the ideas of traditional epistemology together with the new technology, to see how far, if at all, the discipline has to change.

Scepticism

In order to understand the historical roots of modern epistemology, let us begin by asking why Plato studied knowledge in the first place. Plato's opponents in his writings on knowledge were philosophers who were *sceptical* about knowledge, who didn't believe, for some reason, that it was possible to gain knowledge at all.

Such sceptics[4] included the *Sophists* of the fifth century BC, fiercely critical philosophers who tried to explain the universe in terms of the way it appears, rather than by making up theories about what underlies its appearance. Unfortunately, by attracting the ire not only of Plato but Aristotle as well, they garnered a reputation as bloody-minded quibblers more concerned with showing their verbal dexterity than finding the truth, keen to show wrong right and right wrong. They, no doubt, saw themselves as *anti-theorists*, undermining spurious attempts to divine the occult phenomena that supposedly lay behind experience. They were much more interested in the use of argument for practical purposes (e.g., in the law-courts, or in the lively Athenian democracy), rather than for 'pure' metaphysical speculation.

Be that as it may, the Sophists' attack on theories, and on the practical deployment of argument, made them very potent and worthy of

Plato's opposition. There is a lot of power in a theory – think of the status of science and scientists today. In general, sceptics do not try to argue on the theorists' terms (like one scientist arguing that another's experiment was poorly designed in some way), but instead try to suggest that the whole theory itself is unfounded. Nowadays, a space-age Sophist would probably say that if you download a page from the World Wide Web, you might as well take it at face value because there's no way you can reliably find out whether it's true or false. It's an anti-authoritarian gesture; it says that all these expensive scientists and journalists and commentators have no special access to truth. And it has a surface plausibility, in that it is very difficult to ground a theory securely on unimpeachable foundations. If you keep asking, 'but how do you know *that*?', eventually you will get the testy answer, 'I just *do*, that's all!' And when the expensive establishment thinkers get it wrong – in Plato's day, with the decline of Athenian power; in recent times, with the BSE crisis – there is further circumstantial evidence against rooted knowledge/power structures.

In general, scepticism is found attractive as a doctrine by thinkers who worry about glib answers to deep questions, and as a rhetorical device (a stiff test) by those who would hope their theories stand up to the most rigorous scrutiny. Ancient sceptics included Pyrrho, Sextus Empiricus and Cicero; in more modern times scepticism has been used by thinkers as diverse as Montaigne and Descartes, Hume and Hayek. Little wonder that Plato, theorist extraordinaire, deeply opposed the sceptical strain of thought and devoted such a large amount of time to trying to refute it.

Plato and Knowledge: The Birth of Epistemology

Even though we have much of Plato's writing, and even though Plato is a very lucid writer, the actual substance of his thought is not as clear as it might be.[5] For one thing, rather than producing work in the standard form of a treatise or monograph, in which the author sets forward his own view and defends it against counter-argument, Plato wrote *dialogues*. Such dialogues were generally led by Socrates, for whom Plato had great affection,[6] and included other prominent philosophers, Sophists and public figures of the day (typically, the dialogue would be named after one of the participants – Theaetetus, Meno, Gorgias, etc.). Plato – who does not appear – usually, but not always, can be taken as endorsing the views expressed by Socrates. But the dialogues are rarely conclusive, and at the end the participants often agree to differ. In the *Parmenides*, Socrates puts forward arguments that we can confidently attribute to Plato, yet is overwhelmed by Parmenides' criticisms, and the reader is left in little doubt that Parmenides is the moral victor in that one.

Plato's philosophy was not an ivory-tower pursuit without application to the real world. His home city of Athens had recently suffered a terrible reverse in war, amid scandal, corruption and military and naval incompetence. He believed that a properly run city needed a trained class of rulers. Athenian boys were taught how to wrestle or swim; why could they not be taught the virtues appropriate for a good leader? This is a riddle which has always intrigued humanity; indeed, the

English public-school system was one attempt at an answer.

As Plato observed, there are great disputes over the nature of virtue. But if we don't know what virtue *is* – and these disputes imply that we don't – how can we teach it? Many of the early dialogues consist in Socrates demonstrating that his interlocutors do not really *know* what virtue is, and so the question of knowledge – what knowledge of virtue, or anything else for that matter, consists in – loomed large in Plato's work. His ideas changed somewhat over his career, and I don't want to go into the particular details of his epistemological views in this book. But the main point is that he drew an interesting and compelling distinction between *knowledge* and *true belief.*

SOCRATES: *Do you think that knowing and believing are the same, or is there a difference between knowledge and belief?*
GORGIAS: *I should say that there is a difference.*
SOCRATES: *Quite right; and you can prove it like this. If you were asked whether there are*

such things as true and false beliefs, you would say that there are, no doubt.

GORGIAS: *Yes.*

SOCRATES: *But are there such things as true or false knowledge?*

GORGIAS: *Certainly not.*

SOCRATES: *Then knowledge and belief are clearly not the same thing.*

(*Gorgias*, 454cd)[7]

True beliefs are useful, and will not lead you astray. But they are not reliable, in that you could never be sure about them.

SOCRATES: *True opinions are a fine thing, and do all sorts of good so long as they stay in their place; but they will not stay long. They run away from a man's mind, so they are not worth much until you tether them by working out the reason* [why they are true].

(*Meno*, 97e–98a)

Plato spent much effort trying to establish the essential difference between knowledge and true belief, particularly in his great epistemological work, the *Theaetetus*. In that work, Socrates and Theaetetus spend a large part of the middle section comparing knowledge and true belief (187b–201c). The close of the dialogue discusses a theory that knowledge is true belief plus something called a *logos* (201c–210b).

The nature of this *logos* has proved troublesome for philosophers to interpret[8] – it seems to be a sort of explanation or rational account – and anyway Plato does not seem enthused by the idea. The dialogue comes out against the 'knowledge = belief + *logos*' theory. Nevertheless, these discussions and suggestions have been very influential in later philosophy. Knowledge has a reliability that true belief doesn't; to have confidence in your true beliefs, you must give some sort of justification of them. This justification process, whatever it may be, is what turns a belief into knowledge; it makes it *reliable*.

Let us call this analysis of knowledge as 'justified true belief' the 'JTB analysis'.

Other Types of Knowledge

But is all knowledge like this? Using the idea of a belief that happens to be true to point up the essential reliability of knowledge is a nice rhetorical trick, but it doesn't follow that all knowledge is of this form. For surely, some types of knowledge don't really contrast with true *belief* at all. Here are two examples that, at least at first sight, seem to be somewhat different in essence.

- **Know-how.** In Plato's distinction, the difference between knowledge and true belief is that the knowledge can be brought to account. But where know-how is concerned, the contrast is different; the difference between the man who, for example, knows how to drive a car and the man who merely believes he can is that the former can drive a car. If the latter can drive a car as well, then surely he knows how to drive a car; he may believe (and for some reason not know) *that* he can drive a car, but that is a different question. It is not clear, at first sight, that driving a car is a matter of *belief* at all.
- **Bodies of knowledge.** In common idiom, an

encyclopaedia contains knowledge. If there is an agreed interpretation of the words in the book, the interpretation should entail that the words express things that are true and justifiable. But the encyclopaedia has no psychological states at all, and doesn't believe or disbelieve its contents. Beliefs or other psychological states need not come into it.

Why does Plato ignore these types of knowledge? The simple response is that he was chiefly concerned with establishing a distinction between true belief and knowledge, because his diagnosis of the ills of Athens had led him to worry that people were relying complacently on their beliefs about virtue and not seeking knowledge. Those whose beliefs about virtue happened to be true could teach virtue to the next generation; true beliefs don't lead one astray. However, how could it be known whose beliefs were true and whose false? Socrates showed that many of the most confident thinkers were mistaken. For Plato, it all came down to beliefs; other kinds of knowledge, if such there be, weren't the point.

There are more complex reasons, too. For example, with regard to know-how, Plato does discuss expertise in a number of places (e.g., *Theaetetus* 146ce), but he seems to have wanted a definition of knowledge as a single, unified phenomenon, of which different types of expertise would be species. This made it very difficult for him to do full justice to the heterogeneous nature of knowledge.

With regard to bodies of knowledge, Plato was very chary about written-down ideas. He believed that writing was a degenerate form of communication, and this no doubt influenced his adoption of the dialogue form. In the *Phaedrus*, Socrates says:

Writing shares a strange feature with painting. The offspring of painting stand there as if they were alive, but if anyone asks them anything, they are solemnly silent. The same is true of written words. You'd think they were speaking as if they had some understanding, but if you question anything that has been said because you want to learn more, it gives just the same message over and over. Once it has been written down, every discourse rolls about everywhere, reaching just as much those with understanding as those who have no business with it, and it does not know to whom it should speak and to whom not. And when it is faulted and attacked unfairly, it always needs its father's support; alone, it cannot defend itself or come to its own support.

(*Phaedrus*, 275d)

The written is infinitely less interesting to Plato than live discussion. But nowadays technology has blurred the distinction. Some speech – as recorded on TV or radio – is as unchanging as a piece of text. One cannot interact with a recording; it will not change if one debates with it (it 'cannot come to its own support'). One can, of course, debate with the person who made the recording, but the recording will still stand. Like a piece of writing, a recorded utterance will remain in existence even if it has been exposed as a lie, or if its author has changed his mind. Like writing, it can be broadcast to a wide and undiscriminating audience (it 'rolls about everywhere').

None of these things seems particularly controversial to us, but to Plato they were the mark of a degenerate use of language that traded integrity for power. On the other hand, much written language today has speech-like features that Plato would have welcomed. E-mails and text messages allow a certain immediacy of interaction, while dynamically constructed Webpages present information to readers that is customised to their requirements and won't be circulated further.

Of course, there was no reason why Plato should be expected to anticipate such developments. As far as he was concerned, written communication is dead; its author may change his opinions, or the words may be misinterpreted with no way of putting the reader right. But it seems an odd view to hold in the present day, and therefore shouldn't count as a reason why a *modern* epistemologist should be opposed to treating bodies of knowledge as knowledge.[9]

Justified True Belief

I don't want to go into a detailed analysis of Plato's epistemological views (see Further Reading).

The point I want to make is that already, in the first few years of the discipline of epistemology, its general features were in place. In the red corner, a sceptic who denies the possibility of knowledge; in the blue corner, JTB – an idea of knowledge as true belief supplemented by some sort of justification or holding to account. Very few well-known figures in epistemology since have attempted to break the hold of this vision of the debate over knowledge, even though the vision itself was the particular product of Plato's political reaction to a domestic reversal in a Greek city-state nearly two and a half millennia ago. I'll refer to this tradition in epistemology as the 'JTB tradition'.

I will include within the JTB tradition a number of philosophers who do not endorse as such the idea of knowledge as equivalent to justified true belief (as we have noted, this group includes Plato himself – see the *Theaetetus*, 201c–210d), but who follow Plato's general account that knowledge is true belief plus *something*, the 'something' turning 'mere' belief into knowledge. The JTB tradition is therefore firm that knowledge is a *psychological* state, which involves the person with knowledge assenting to or endorsing a *proposition*.

There is huge dispute amongst philosophers about what a proposition actually is, but for our purposes we can ignore this issue, because all are agreed that a proposition is expressed by a declarative sentence (i.e., one that says something about the world, not a question, command etc.). So propositional knowledge is knowledge *that* something or other is the case. And this does look very like a belief – an attitude towards a proposition.

For example, Sir A.J. Ayer devotes a whole chapter of his theory of knowledge to examining various different types, only to decide in the end – on the basis of what appears to be not very much – that knowledge is JTB after all.[10] Susan Haack moves straight into an impressive examination of the justification of beliefs (though in fairness it should be said that this is an interesting philosophical issue in its own right).[11]

Away from the mainstream, the American philosopher Fred Dretske tries to avoid the JTB definition, and instead analyses knowledge in terms of the information that caused the belief.[12] This is potentially a helpful move (as we shall see later on) but in this particular formulation doesn't get us very far. It is still the case that (a) something is known only when it is believed, (b) someone only knows something when they believe it, (c) what is known is true, and (d) it has a justification (in terms of information theory). In an important new work, Timothy Williamson breaks radically with the JTB *characterisation*, but stays within the JTB *tradition* by setting out from the assumption that knowing is a state of mind, and that knowing something in general entails believing it.[13] Even Wittgenstein continues to think primarily of beliefs, and sees his chief opponent as an epistemological sceptic.[14]

Nicholas Everitt and Alec Fisher (see Further Reading) produce a thorough survey of the efforts of philosophers to define the 'something extra',[15] but are forced to conclude that there is still, after two and a half millennia, no final consensus:

[W]e have learned that there is universal agreement that knowledge requires truth. Secondly,

there is an almost equally widespread agreement
that knowledge requires belief. The disagreement
arises on what more is required for knowledge
than true belief.[16]

Surely another option open to us is to reject the
analysis as a whole and step outside the JTB
tradition. This is a radical step in the face of
universal agreement. Why make it? Is there any
reason for us to do it?

The Sceptic Bites Back

First of all, the animus of the JTB tradition has
usually been focused on the sceptic. As we have
seen, Plato was at least in part responding to sceptics, but scepticism can be much more thoroughgoing than that of Plato's opponents, Sophists
such as Protagoras or quasi-Sophists like Gorgias.
The earliest, really dedicated sceptic in intellectual history was Arcesilaus (*c.* 315–*c.* 240 BC),
the first man who was positively in favour of
withdrawing belief – and once you start question-
ing absolutely everything, it is not difficult to
win arguments by destroying your opponent's

position without advancing any positive thesis yourself.

At the basic level, everyone has wondered how they know they are not currently dreaming. René Descartes (1596–1650) famously tried to build philosophy on unassailable foundations by conducting a fictitious argument with a very bloody-minded sceptic who doubted everything; the attempt, sadly, foundered on the fact that most observers agree that the sceptic rather won the day. Indeed – I blush – even I once managed to prove, on the basis of some fairly innocuous premises, that everybody was dreaming all of the time![17]

It made sense for Plato to aim his arguments at sceptics, as they were prominent in Athenian political life at the time. It is less so for modern-day epistemologists, for no one occupies the sceptical position, except within academia. There are other purposes for epistemology, and other people who are interested in the arguments. Given the changing intellectual background, surely it would be better to reject scepticism as a type of philosophical disease (with Wittgenstein –

see Note 14), and focus epistemological efforts on the areas where they can do some good and make a difference in the world.

Information Overload

When Plato was writing, scepticism was a serious political problem. Nowadays it is not. But his genius and lucidity have combined to cast a spell over the JTB tradition, and the same issues that preoccupied Plato are still being investigated, even though conditions have changed. Technological, economic and political developments that Plato could never have foreseen mean that epistemological theory needs to deal with different phenomena, and many epistemological assumptions could usefully be amended. 'The nature of knowledge cannot survive unchanged within this context of general transformation.'[18]

The new world to which epistemology needs to be applied is characterised by a dramatic increase in the quantity of *data* that are being created and stored, as storage capacity has multiplied and cost diminished. When Plato was writing, the space required to store a work written on a scroll was large, the cost of reproducing it huge. Bound books reduced that space, and, once printing allowed the production of millions of volumes, libraries could hold them. Now, a floppy disk will hold a decent-sized book, a CD-ROM even more, and a laptop computer still more. More books are being written, and more periodicals published. More photographs are being taken, X-rays shot, videos made.

And the cost of storing all this material has shrunk rapidly. The new British Library in London, designed to hold 12 million volumes, cost £500 million. But magnetic storage is a different matter. A byte is the amount of storage required for a single character, so a book is 1 million bytes, or a megabyte. A gigabyte is the standard measure of data, a thousand megabytes (i.e., a thousand books). And the cost of storing a gigabyte of data magnetically was not much more than £5 in late 2000, and will be well under £1 by 2005, when the virtual equivalent of the British Library will cost a mere £12,000.

The opportunities this new technology has brought are already being exploited. To begin with, very little of the new material recorded in the world appears in print. As a consequence, the production of data has been 'democratised', in that most new stuff is created by individuals for a small audience: for example, office documents (80 per cent of all new paper documents), photographs (95 per cent of film documents) and camcorder tapes (20 per cent of magnetic tape storage). And it is the magnetically stored documents that are increasing in number; the use of paper and film for original content is remaining more or less constant.

Hence, whereas even 20 years ago the amount of data accessed (and created) by the ordinary citizen was relatively small, nowadays anyone living in a developed economy, with computers, electricity and reliable telephone or wireless connections, can get hold of colossal quantities of material, and can author a pretty huge amount as well. In all, as estimated by Hal Varian, humankind creates round about 1 exabyte of data annually. That is 1 *billion* gigabytes, or 1,000,000,000,000 books.

Which is not too far off 200 books' worth of

data for every man, woman and child on the planet! Every *single* year![19]

This is not a world with which we, as yet, feel comfortable. We can all remember when people were starved of information; now we are drowning in it. If people had little or no access to the data they needed in the past, now we all know the feeling of having to trawl through pages and pages, documents and documents, to find just the exact thing we need. Having more data has not solved all our information requirements. It has merely given us *information overload*.

Will it be possible to deal more efficiently and intelligently with all these data? There are grounds for saying that it will. To see why, let's take a look at one of the influential technologies of the information revolution, the Internet.

The Internet and the World Wide Web

We all know the outer forms of the Internet: e-mails, the Web, newsgroups etc. We know we can contact our friends, do our banking through it, buy books or CDs. Some people say it will change our lives; others that it will make no difference at all. It is extraordinary, though, how few commentators are actually aware of the technology, and how prosaic it is.

The Internet is simply a network of computer networks, connected using the *Internet Protocol* (IP). IP enables a computer to take a file, break it up into slices called *packets*, and then send the packets to a destination (another computer) down a phone line using *dynamic routing* (i.e., making up routes to the destination, via various intermediaries, while the packets are in transit). Dynamic routing was a Cold War idea – if the intermediate computers were knocked out by enemy action, another route could be created. In practice, dynamic routing is useful in peacetime as it can steer packets around more standard equipment failures. The *Transmission Control Protocol* (TCP) tracks the packets, and the combination of protocols – the Internet standard – is called TCP/IP.

The public face of the Internet, most responsible for the Internet's take-off, is that fraction of the net called the *World Wide Web* (WWW or *the Web*). This is, in effect, a vast collection of files in multiple media – text, pictures, sounds, video, and so on. The Web works by storing the files on many different computers, called *servers*. It 'pretends' that the files on it are stored at a single source, by having a consistent system of addresses for the files, called *Uniform Resource Locators* (URL), which is what you type in the address box of your browser (the software that gives you a view of the Web, such as Internet Explorer, or Netscape Navigator). For example, the URL of Icon Books' Website is http://www.iconbooks.co.uk. Your computer gets at the file held at that URL by using (usually) the *Hypertext Transfer Protocol*, which is what the 'http' stands for. The use of HTTP makes it possible to access files stored anywhere in the world as if they were all held on a single giant host computer.

What makes the Web possible is its universal language, the *Hypertext Markup Language* (HTML), which structures a file so that your computer can lay out its data in the browser window, while also allowing it to contain links to other files – these are the *hyperlinks* generally highlighted in blue in a piece of text.

Clicking on such links allows your computer to get at another file at another URL. Well-designed hyperlinks let you navigate through the Web looking at only the particular files you are interested in, unlike a standard text or video, where the structure is linear and you cannot easily hop about as you wish. HTML is an international standard, not owned by a particular company, and administered by the World Wide Web Consortium (W3C), which helps the Web to be open both to readers *and* writers.

The openness of HTML allows pretty well anyone to create content and post it on the Web. The result has been an explosion of data. There are about 2.5 billion fixed documents on the Web, and when you add in all the databases that users can access through forms to create customised Webpages (e.g., the files that allow you to log on to your bank and see your own bank statements), that figure rises to 550 billion documents.

This is a huge amount of material (7.5 million gigabytes of data = 7,500,000,000 books). And this is just the Web; the Internet is far more than that! Needless to say, it is an unprecedented amount of information for people to have access to instantaneously. And it is this that has made the Internet the engine for a colossal shift in human capabilities.

Some commentators have refused to see the Internet as a significant enough change in technology to make it philosophically interesting; others have worried that the Internet will only bring problems. It is certainly important not to overstate the case for the defence, particularly in a world where half the population has never made a telephone call.[20] However, the sudden explosion of available content could be as significant to human development as the invention of movable type. As we have seen in this section, the actual technological developments aren't earth-shattering; a few transfer protocols here, a markup language there, and a system for managing changes and addresses. But, as with printing, a number of small changes, taken cumulatively, could have major effects.[21]

Knowledge, Technology and Organisations

Many of the Internet's small changes will be central to the knowledge economy. They will enable organisations to disperse knowledge across their members (employees, representatives, etc). This is essential – if knowledge is the key to competitive advantage, as we saw at the beginning of this book, then it has to be used well and efficiently by organisations.

Can an organisation *possess* knowledge? Does it make sense to say that? Recall that the JTB tradition in epistemology says that knowing is a *psychological* state, that it is something done only by people.

Well, there is certainly one uncontroversial way in which an organisation can be said to possess knowledge (possibly metaphorically), and that is if it employs someone who unambiguously has that knowledge. Let us imagine a fictitious firm, Worldwide Manufacturing; suppose it makes a particular type of widget, type X, and it employs Smith, an expert in X, in its London office. Then we can say that Worldwide Manufacturing contains or possesses knowledge about X, in this case in the person of Smith. If Smith goes, Worldwide Manufacturing would no longer contain that knowledge. This is pretty straightforward at this stage – nothing about the situation contradicts the JTB theory.

Now consider a second stage. WM executives realise that Smith is a scarce resource – he goes on holiday, he sleeps at night, he has coffee breaks, all of which mean that his expertise is not always available. Furthermore, he is based in London, whereas WM is a multinational; if something goes wrong with their X-factory in São Paolo, it will at best be difficult to employ Smith's expertise, with time differences, logistical problems of getting the knowledge from London to São Paolo in time, and a language problem – Smith speaks no Portuguese.

As a result, WM undertakes a *knowledge acquisition* exercise. This involves specialists interviewing Smith and creating a system that apes his expertise in X. This could be a computer system, but we will suppose it is a set of interlinked Webpages designed to mimic Smith's problem-solving behaviour. If something goes wrong on the X-assembly line, the manager can look up the appropriate page, which will tell him or her what to do. When there are different possibilities, there will be a choice of links to take the user to the appropriate page. The way the user *navigates* through the set of Webpages will track the way that Smith diagnoses problems in X and sorts them out. These Webpages can then be posted on WM's corporate *Intranet* (i.e., a private section of the Internet, accessible only with a password), and so – via an automatic translation system – are immediately accessible to the non-experts in São Paolo and elsewhere who need to know about X. They will also be accessible to people in London who might need Smith's expertise after office hours or during his holidays.

After this second stage, we can still say that WM contains Smith's knowledge. Smith works for WM, as at the first stage. It is just that WM is more efficient about sending Smith's knowledge around the firm.

But now consider a third stage, when Smith retires, or is poached by WM's rivals. WM does not have to stop making X-type widgets; neither does it have to employ a new expert. Smith's expertise is still available to engineers 24 hours a day, seven days a week, as long as they have a laptop and a phone line. The Intranet is still running the Webpages about X-type widgets, and their navigation structure causes the user to go through the same problem-solving process that Smith would have gone through.

Now, earlier on, we used the phrase, 'WM contains knowledge about X', loosely, metaphorically, knowing there was an easy rationalisation of it, since Smith was an employee of WM. Now, however, we cannot be so loose, because Smith has left. No person within the organisation has Smith's problem-solving capability. The people who drew up the Webpages were most likely independent consultants who have long since gone; let us further suppose that nothing has ever gone wrong with an X-type widget, and that therefore no one in WM has ever even read the Webpages. No one in WM has any justified true beliefs about problems with X-type widgets.

And yet, it is very intuitive to say that WM still

contains, or possesses the knowledge about, X. If there is any difficulty with an X-type widget in Brazil or England or Russia or India or Nigeria, the WM engineer on the spot will be able to find out from WM's corporate Intranet exactly what to do. The knowledge available for the engineer is so much more than he or she would get from a book about X, in that the engineer, together with the links that organise the Intranet, will solve the problem. The engineer need not read all the Webpages; instead it is the *organisation of the Website* that provides the expertise that previously Smith used to provide.

It looks like we would have to say that any epistemology that is to be *applicable* in this context should allow for *organisations* as well as people possessing knowledge in a non-metaphorical way. It would certainly be possible for an alternative analysis to be developed, or the JTB tradition defended (see the final section); but epistemology will be that much more valuable in the knowledge economy if epistemologists take its concerns seriously, and don't try to analyse them away. As Lyotard puts it:

We may thus expect a thorough exteriorization of knowledge with respect to the 'knower,' at whatever point he or she may occupy in the knowledge process. The old principle that the acquisition of knowledge is indissociable from the training of minds, or even of individuals, is becoming obsolete ... The relationship of the suppliers and users of knowledge to the knowledge they supply and use is now tending ... to assume the form already taken by the relationship of commodity producers and consumers to the commodities they produce and consume – that is, the form of value.[22]

And indeed, we shouldn't end this section without noting that in the social sciences, treating an organisation as an agent in its own right, greater than the sum of the people who make up that organisation, with its own goals, methods and values, would not be unusual. The JTB tradition would need an update to retain consistency with such thinking.[23]

Managing Knowledge

The knowledge possessed by an organisation is an *asset* of that organisation. I mean by this that the knowledge is a claim on future benefits. The organisation *invests* money in the acquisition of a knowledge asset (e.g., by beginning a programme of research and development) in the hope that this investment will pay dividends by increasing future effectiveness (or profits, in the case of a firm).

Like any asset, the knowledge an organisation possesses needs to be managed properly in order to realise the anticipated benefits. This is where the insights of epistemology will be of enormous value, as an understanding of the properties and dynamics of knowledge is essential to knowing how best to use knowledge for an organisation's general benefit.

An example: on 23 August 2001, the famous pottery company Royal Doulton announced a half-yearly loss of £9 million and placed its factories on a four-day week; its shares had fallen to a fifth of their 1998 value. One major factor in its decline was that it had failed to spot trends in the ceramics market. For instance, over the last few years, British diners have abandoned the big family dinner in favour of TV dinners, meals out, meals *al fresco*, and generally more casual dining. However, Doulton had continued to produce sets of matching china, rather than individual pieces available at supermarkets and other convenient outlets. It did not know what its customers wanted; its half-yearly report admitted to 'weaknesses in its information systems'.

What is going on? Doulton employs about 3,000 people in Stoke-on-Trent, almost all of whom will have been well aware of – indeed part of – the trend away from set-piece meals. Poor *management* of that knowledge, possessed by nearly all of its employees, meant that the changes in dining patterns were never taken account of by management. As a result, the company made losses, and people's jobs are at risk.[24]

What sorts of issue are involved in managing knowledge? A recent UK scientific research project, Advanced Knowledge Technologies (AKT), has characterised knowledge management as six challenges. These are as follows – and to show that they are not merely management issues, I have annotated them with meaty and classic epistemological questions, given in italics.

- **Acquisition.** The initial problem with knowledge is when and how to acquire it. We can distinguish three levels of acquisition. First, there is knowledge that currently does not exist and would have to be discovered by a programme of research (e.g., a cure for AIDS). Second, there is knowledge that exists, but is not possessed by the organisation. Third, there is knowledge that is possessed by the organisation, but in the wrong form (e.g., in our example from the previous section, Smith's knowledge of X-type widgets was held inconveniently in his head, and a decision to acquire the knowledge from him and place it in a set of Webpages was taken). The management decisions here depend on the difficulty of acquiring the knowledge (does a suitable code exist?), the costs of the acquisition, and the projected benefits. *How can we know what we don't know? How can we know what we need* *to know? How can different types of know-ledge be justified?*

- **Modelling.** Once acquired, knowledge has to be stored in a useful way. The representation must be such that it is easy to write the knowledge down as it comes in, and equally easy to read the knowledge once it is acquired. *How should different types of knowledge best be represented? How far does changing a representation change the knowledge?*

- **Retrieval.** When an organisation has a large repository of knowledge, it must be possible to get at the knowledge quickly enough for it to be of use. This means that the repository must be structured to allow a quick, reliable and efficient search of its contents. If the knowledge disappears in a pile of other stuff – like the Ark of the Covenant in the final scene of *Raiders of the Lost Ark* – it is as good as forgotten. *How best to organise connected pieces of knowledge? How do they relate to each other?*

- **Re-use.** If some knowledge is present in a firm, people who need that knowledge need to know how to get hold of it, so they don't go about re-acquiring knowledge expensively (or incompetently, like Royal Doulton). *How do we recognise knowledge that we need and don't have? How do pieces of knowledge relate to each other?*

- **Publishing.** It is essential that the people who need knowledge get it at the right time. Too soon, and it contributes to their information overload; too late, and ... well, it's too late. They also need it in the right form. Someone who needs one little piece of technical information does not need either a whole set of explanations for beginners or a highly rarefied piece of theory. *Does changing the way knowledge is visualised change the knowledge? How do we know what we need to know?*

- **Maintenance.** Having developed a repository of knowledge, it has to be kept running and up to date. This involves a series of disparate issues, such as: verifying that the knowledge is correct, and that the representation correctly represents the knowledge; updating the knowledge to keep track of changes in the domain; 'forgetting' knowledge that is misleading or out of date; altering formats as the organisation's needs change; maybe even packaging and selling the knowledge if it would be valuable for outsiders. *How do we know that an account of the world is correct? How do we know that a sentence correctly represents a proposition? What is the logical relation between statements, and how can the effects of the removal of a statement be tracked? How can different types of knowledge be justified?*[25]

These challenges all involve epistemological problems, many of which have long been the object of study in traditional epistemology, others of which are new, still others old problems with newly acquired significance. But this is a context where the application of epistemology would be extremely timely. The problems of scepticism, which have driven so much epistemological research, are very much less pressing.

Data, Information and Knowledge

Is this to say that everything that appears on the Internet, or in corporate disk space, is to be called knowledge? Is every item in a symbolic code knowledge – even those items that are unreadable or useless?

Of course, that is not the idea. What we want to sort out is which items are worthy of epistemological investigation. We will focus on computer-based items, although the same distinctions that we are about to draw will apply to paper-based materials, and even to thoughts and beliefs.

Let us begin by examining the basic content in a computer – a set of symbols; we can call this **data**. Data can be any old garbage, and so may be useful or may not. A subclass of data we can call **information**, which is those data that have an *interpretation*, or which make *sense*. Of course, the attribution of meaning to something is a deep and complex philosophical problem in itself, but let's assume that we can draw some sort of a distinction between meaningless stuff and meaningful stuff. In the case of Webpages, meaningful stuff can of course include pictures and video, as well as text.

How might information contrast with knowledge? Let's try to suggest a distinction by the use of an example.

For several years now, supermarkets have recorded the details of each purchase made in them by using electronic tills, each of which updates a central database. As a result, supermarkets with nationwide chains of branches have enormous masses of data about billions and billions of purchases. These data are clearly information, as the big databanks will have some interpretation which enables the reader to work out which purchase is referred to, what was purchased, how much it cost, etc.

Is this vast quantity of information useful in itself? Hardly. No human reader could scan the printouts in a lifetime, even if he wanted to, still less draw any conclusions from it. If such stuff is knowledge, then there doesn't seem to be much point in having it.

However, one can imagine converting such data-sets into knowledge (this would be a knowledge acquisition process, in the terms of the previous section). Using special computer programs called *machine learning programs*, or *induction programs*, a computer can trawl through enormous data-sets and extract statistical relationships between some of the data. These relationships can then be published as sets of rules, which might look something like:

- People in Hertfordshire spend more per visit to the supermarket than people in Berkshire.

- People in Inner London who buy beer are more likely to buy crisps simultaneously.

- People in the South-West have become keener on branded tinned food over the last five years.

What I would like to suggest now is that these probabilistic inductions are not only information but **knowledge**. They are knowledge because they are *usable*, because they can be translated into *effective action*. They are not, let's face it, terribly exciting, but they will help a supermarket save money on deliveries, warehousing and marketing by sending goods where they are most likely to be sold quickly. It is not an exact science, by any means, but there is some payoff for this sort of activity, and it would not be possible without the collection of the giant data-sets through the electronic tills.

Note further that none of this need ever appear as anyone's *belief*. The content of the data-sets is obviously collected independently of any human operator. The machine learning program will extract the knowledge without consulting anyone. And the knowledge thus extracted might easily be translated into managerial actions (e.g., changes in orders of wholesale goods) automatically, without any human managerial interference.

And it is knowledge of this sort that organisations such as supermarkets have to manage. There is an investment in the collection of those data and in running the hardware and software that makes it possible, and organisations need to know whether the investment is worth it. The reader can satisfy himself or herself that the six challenges of knowledge management will apply here. Dealing effectively with bodies of knowledge of this sort will make a big difference to the profits of commercial firms and to the success of non-commercial organisations.

So, let's recap our characterisation. Data are sets of symbols, while information is meaningful data. Knowledge is that information which is usable for the purposes of supporting or suggesting action; it is a stepping stone to some end.

Data, information, knowledge: they sit as a pyramid. Perhaps, with tongue only slightly in cheek, one might even imagine wisdom sitting at the apex, characterised as the ability to select appropriate important goals for one's useful knowledge to be applied to.

Scepticism is out of place here. The supermarket of our example wants help with the six challenges of knowledge management. A proof that, say, the external world exists and that the five senses can deliver knowledge, reassuring and philosophically interesting though this may be, is not going to be of any help in deciding how many tins of beans to send to Wiltshire. The manager who doubted the existence of Wiltshire would be given a long rest, not a proof.

The Semantic Web

This characterisation of knowledge – as usable information – has been generally adopted by those researching knowledge management in the Internet age. By creating technologies that help in the handling of information, more information becomes usable, and therefore by our criteria, turns from information to knowledge. Hence technologists, such as W3C, or the AKT project mentioned above, who have taken the 'usable information' characterisation on board, can produce real systems and tools that actively help organisations and individuals become more effective by controlling the information they have access to. Information overload is alleviated, not by reducing the amount of information available, but by increasing the amount of knowledge.

W3C has developed a language for writing Webpages to supersede HTML, a language called XML (eXtensible Markup Language – actually a language for representing other languages, but let's steer clear of details!). XML allows designers to place 'tags' in Webpages that are invisible to the reader (i.e., they don't appear in the browser when the Webpage is being read), but which *can* be read by a computer. These tags can then 'tell' the user's computer what the number or the word is about. Contrast this with HTML, which simply tells the computer where to place the data on-screen.

A browser that is XML-enabled (i.e., can cope with XML) will be able to search not just for key words on the page but also taking into account their underlying meaning, as represented by the tags. So, whereas currently a search engine will come up with, say, 10,000 hits, with XML it might come up with only 20 hits, but they will be the 20 you want, because they will be tagged with the subject area of your interest. If your interest is in Kate Bush, then typing in 'Bush' together with some specification of your musical requirements, the engine will ignore all the George Bushes, Shepherd's Bushes, rose bushes, African bushes, etc. The new search will be much more sensitive to the *context* of the query.

That in itself would give the user of the Internet much more control of the information received. As it stands, XML is a comparative infant, but telling computers what Webpages are about is an idea that will surely be exploited in a large number of currently undreamt-of ways. The interpretation of Web-based text and images, currently a human responsibility, could at least partly be done automatically. This will allow projects like AKT to write software that can provide information (e.g., flight information) and world-altering services (e.g., ticket-buying agents), ushering in *context-sensitive knowledge services* – ways of providing people and organisations with the technology to solve their particular knowledge problems as they happen, and as they need solutions.

Most of these services would ordinarily be done by a person – the difference is not that new work gets done, but that it gets done quickly, automatically, in a standard way, and exhaustively (i.e., an agent can search the entire Web for the best price for an air ticket, in a fraction of a second). Information overload would be alleviated by the reduction of routine tasks, and the standardisation of non-routine tasks.

This conception of the World Wide Web

augmented by XML is called the *Semantic Web*, and is based entirely on the new characterisation of knowledge. Without the recognition of the epistemological importance of usable information, such a conception might never have arisen. It certainly has nothing to do with JTB. Many of these developments will seem small-scale and technical, but they are powerful and cumulatively important, and they would not have come about without the change in approach to the problem of knowledge.

Knowledge: Justified?

So, we have established a rival conception of knowledge, and furthermore one that has been the driver of important developments in technology. What is the relationship between the 'usable information' conception of knowledge and the JTB tradition?

One thing that has often been remarked upon in the history of epistemology is that the nature of the justification of a belief sufficient to convert it to knowledge (or the 'something extra' required in the stead of justification) is highly problematic. Even leaving aside some fiendish thought experiments developed by Edmund Gettier in the 1960s that cast doubt on any reasonable notion of justification as being sufficient – experiments which no one has satisfactorily explained away – there has never been any consensus about what justification would do.[26]

Even under the 'usable information' characterisation, some sort of justification of the knowledge's efficacy would be required. The quality of a stock-control system will affect a firm's profits and its employees' jobs; the quality of a heart-monitoring system will affect a person's chances of life. In such sensitive contexts, the knowledge that has been put into the computer had better be reliable.

But there is a difference in the role of the justification under the two characterisations. In the JTB tradition, the justification is central – a true belief is knowledge if and only if the justification of the belief is adequate. Philosophers have suggested a number of possible types of justification. Examples include: the knowledge can be derived from some privileged, deep foundational knowledge from which all knowledge must spring; the knowledge was discovered using reliable techniques; the knowledge is part of a coherent picture of the world. There is no consensus about which, if any, is correct.

Under the 'usable information' view, on the other hand, a justification is a kind of certificate that the knowledge could be the basis for action of some type. It would be the proof that the information being discussed was usable. However, the existence of the proof would be required, not to turn the information into knowledge, but to demonstrate that the information was usable and reliable. Often, of course, usability requires a demonstration of reliability – as with computers in sensitive contexts. But the existence of a justification, or proof, or anything extra over and above the usefulness of the information, is not *conceptually* bound up with the identification of information with knowledge.

Interestingly, Plato discusses the possibility of such a pragmatic definition of knowledge in the *Theaetetus* 167ab. The idea that epistemologists might be concerned with which knowledge is

worth knowing – as opposed to which knowledge is legitimised by various different technical
accounts of knowledge – has not been pursued
much since, but Plato does give the issue pro-
found thought in the *Theaetetus* 172b–177c. (He
would no doubt disagree with our conclusions
here, though.)

Knowledge: True?

Usable information that is propositional will
(usually if not all the time) be true. In our supermarket example, if the propositions induced by
the machine-learning program (e.g., that people
in Hertfordshire spend more, etc.) actually turn
out to be false, the supermarket will make poor
decisions based on this misinformation. Its acting
on these false propositions will be likely, all else
being equal, to reduce its profits. Hence, the
information will not be usable in the way
required by our characterisation; it will not be
able to underlie *effective* action.

Does this mean that all knowledge is true acc-
ording to our characterisation? Recall that this is
universally agreed in traditional epistemology

(Everitt and Fisher, pp. 48–9). Does the new episte-mology that we are proposing here fall in with the consensus?

The answer, interestingly, is 'no': one can act effectively on information that is not strictly true.

To take an initial and obvious example: much of the knowledge that is required in industry is know-how rather than propositional knowledge. It is knowledge that can help achieve something. Hence it is of an imperative form (first do *this*, then *this*, then *this*, if you want to achieve *that*), rather than the propositional form (*this* is the case), which is more usually associated with truth and falsity. The imperative form can be useful or not useful, appropriate or inappropriate, but not strictly true or false.

A second example of knowledge that is not true is what is called *default* reasoning. We rely on default reasoning to an enormous degree in our problem-solving. The idea of default reasoning is that you can treat generalisations as universally true, even when they are not. So, for example, when told that Tweety is a bird, we deduce that Tweety flies, based on our knowledge that all birds fly. The reasoning is sound. Only one problem: it is not true that all birds fly (penguins and ostriches don't, for a start), and if we later find out that Tweety happens to be a penguin, then we will withdraw the conclusion that he flies. This is default reasoning.

In general, default reasoning has been ignored by philosophers (with honourable exceptions). It was first properly examined by computer scientists trying to develop machines with artificial intelligence, who were faced by the practical realisation that default reasoning is used all the time.[27] We blithely assume that all elephants are grey, all rooms have floors, all cars have four wheels, all tigers have four legs, all chairs can be sat on, all restaurants charge customers for food, etc. These propositions are all false (it is not true that *all* rooms have floors, because when my house was being renovated, the kitchen had no floor; and so on with the other examples). But surely, if we know anything, it is that rooms have floors. The information provided by these propositions – the essential inferences they allow us to make – justifies this conclusion.

A third example is that of *heuristic* reasoning. This is reasoning by rule of thumb, and is a vital part of the knowledge of experts in particular fields (i.e., of *expertise*). Much expertise consists of getting the right answer quickly with the minimum of investigation. For example, given a medical dictionary and a functioning laboratory most of us could diagnose an illness eventually. The problem would be that it would take so long, the patient would probably be dead by the time we knew what he had. The expert diagnostician, on the other hand, has to pinpoint the disease quickly enough to treat it. In order to achieve that speed, the diagnostician will bundle together a lump of medical knowledge into a quick-and-dirty rule, which will tell him that, for example, if a patient has a white-blood-cell count of x, and a certain set of antibodies present, he probably has a disease from a particular class. This is a *heuristic*, and is literally false, in that the patient could have that particular white-blood-cell count and that particular antibody and yet not have the disease. Clearly, heuristic reasoning is related to default reasoning; the distinction is that the heuristics are less likely to be borne out by events. They are not deep-down assumptions but clever shortcuts developed professionally as part of the execution of expertise.

Each of these types of information, I am claiming, should be seen as knowledge, in that they are all extremely usable for effective action. Everyone uses know-how and default reasoning; experts rely on heuristics. Can an epistemologist possibly ignore these?

Knowledge: Belief?

Perhaps the most radical departure I am proposing is that knowledge need not be a psychological state. There are philosophers who are prepared to take a smaller step, that knowledge isn't a belief; for example, Timothy Williamson (see Note 13). The requirements of the Internet age, however, are stronger than that. Knowledge does not have to be anything psychological at all.

As we have seen from the widget example earlier, from the point of view of an organisation and its need to manage its knowledge effectively to get the maximum benefit from it, there is no essential difference between the organisation possessing knowledge via its employees, and its possessing it via some artificial means (e.g., an Intranet, manuals, organisational procedures, etc.).

Seen from the JTB tradition, the widget example changes radically as we go through the various stages. When there is an expert on X-type widgets in the firm, there is a (merely) metaphorical sense in which the firm can be said to possess the knowledge; when the expert leaves, then there is no person within the firm with any knowledge; the two situations are completely different. *This surely renders the JTB tradition useless from the point of view of those who need to understand and manage their knowledge in an organisational context.* Epistemologically, the organisation is interested only in its capabilities, not in how those capabilities are manifested. In other words, it is the 'belief' element of JTB, rather than the 'justified' or 'true' bit, that has most to do with rendering the JTB tradition ineffective as a tool for understanding the requirements of the knowledge economy which we set out at the beginning of this book.

Conclusion: Twenty-first Century Alchemy?

To review our analysis, we have examined the JTB tradition in the context of the knowledge economy, and found it wanting. An epistemology suitable for this technological climate can be fairly relaxed about justification; knowledge should be justified, but different types of knowledge will need different types of justification. The requirement for truth needs to be replaced with a requirement for effectiveness (which will, one imagines, coincide with truth to a large extent). The analysis of knowledge as a belief, or as any psychological state, seriously undermines the JTB tradition in the modern context.

The proposal is that the JTB characterisation be replaced by the characterisation of knowledge as 'usable information'. We have illustrated the ideas here, although of course what has transpired in this book falls a long way short of a tight definition. No doubt, giving such a definition to the new conception of knowledge will be as difficult as the task of refining the JTB conception has been. However, technologists such as W3C and

AKT have been able to use 'usable information' as a practical guide to understanding the problems of knowledge management, and developing technologies that can help alleviate those problems.

There are responses that a philosopher of the JTB tradition can make. A *heroic response* asserts that the traditional analysis of knowledge defines what knowledge is, and therefore usable information cannot be knowledge (however interesting or important it may be). This, in effect, says that whatever problems there are in the knowledge economy, *we're* not going to help you with them.

There is no argument against this response, of course; it is perfectly self-consistent. But we have seen from the account of the knowledge management challenges that there are serious and interesting epistemological problems associated with them, and it would be disappointing were our cry for help refused.

More constructive is an *analytic response* which would review our examples and try to show that they 'really' are examples of JTB in some way or other. For example, this response would attempt to show that some of our 'false' knowledge is really true when you understand it properly, or that what seem to be non-beliefs are actually reducible to psychological states in some way.

Though it takes our concerns more seriously, this isn't a great improvement on the heroic response. Its underlying premise, that epistemology is more or less okay once we realise that we have misconstrued the significance of our 'counter-examples', fails to take into account the essential need for experts to reach out to their constituency, rather than the other way round. An expert, whether an epistemologist, physicist, astrologer or car mechanic, must tailor his or her expertise to the people who need it, not vice versa. It is not for the busy corporate executive or NGO director to try to fit their knowledge problems into the JTB framework; rather, it is the job of the epistemologist to show how the JTB theory applies to the problems as they appear on the ground. Any devious analysis is, in a sense, the 'hidden wiring' that the user of the theory must not be bothered with.

But, if we are to face up to the facts, the Internet and related technological innovations have changed the way knowledge is viewed. In Plato's day, when the JTB tradition began, knowledge was a personal accomplishment, and so it continued pretty well up to the present. But there has been a gradual change, so that knowledge is now also a commodity, to be bought, sold, managed, invested in, leveraged, deployed, etc. We need an epistemology appropriate for this context, and the JTB tradition isn't it.

Of course, I have been describing a world of new technology and buzzwords that may be a passing fad. It may be thought that if JTB sits tight and ignores present circumstances, it will regain its applicability. This is certainly possible, but doesn't detract from the need for an information-based epistemology now, and the mere fact that the knowledge economy may disappear next week shows neither that it has no pressing epistemological requirements, nor that any epistemological discoveries made in that context will have no wider interest or application.

In short, there is a need for an epistemology

tailored for a specific audience which the JTB tradition has failed to deliver, and it is in danger of missing a real opportunity to move from academe into a constructive engagement with the world of commerce and technology.

It may be that epistemology now is in the position of the philosophy of matter in the late medieval period. Philosophers had always had theories of what the world was made of, from the times of the ancient Greeks to the alchemists, and these theories came under the heading of 'natural philosophy'. However, in the seventeenth century, particularly thanks to Newton, natural philosophy gradually acquired an empirical basis, and found itself debating, not antiquated thought experiments about how far you could divide space or substance, but problems such as the correct description of the orbits of the planets. It is certainly not the case that the alchemists made no contribution to our understanding of matter, but it cannot be denied that if you want to find out about what makes up our world, you would be wiser to ask a physicist or a chemist. Natural philosophy gradually transmuted into hard science.

There are resemblances between epistemology now and natural philosophy then. After millennia of relatively inconclusive debate, there is for the first time a basis and a requirement for empirical application of ideas. Some of these ideas will be of great use in this new world, others will turn out to be useless. My guess, and I can't say I know this, is that the JTB tradition will turn out to be a dead end – the alchemy of our day.

Notes

1. There are many works defending this switch to the 'new' economy. For instance, Thomas A. Stewart, *Intellectual Capital: The New Wealth of Organizations* (London: Nicholas Brealey Publishing, 1997), Leif Edvinsson and Michael S. Malone, *Intellectual Capital* (London: Piatkus, 1997), Thomas H. Davenport and Laurence Prusak, *Working Knowledge: How Organizations Manage What They Know* (Boston: Harvard Business School Press, 1997). A more philosophical analysis is Jean-François Lyotard, *The Postmodern Condition: A Report on Knowledge* (Manchester: Manchester University Press, 1984).

2. See Joseph Stiglitz, 'Scan Globally, Reinvent Locally: Knowledge Infrastructure and the Localisation of Knowledge', in Diane Stone (ed.), *Banking on Knowledge: The Genesis of the Global Development Network* (London: Routledge, 2000), pp. 24–43, and other papers in that volume.

3. Alan Burton-Jones, *Knowledge Capitalism: Business, Work and Learning in the New Economy* (Oxford: Oxford University Press, 1999), pp. 8–9.

4. I am using the term 'sceptic' loosely here to describe anyone who, for whatever reason, doubted the veracity of objective knowledge. 'Sceptic' can also denote, in a more narrow sense, particular schools of philosophy such as the Pyrrhonists and the Academic sceptics (of whom Cicero was one).

5. I am not, in this book, going to supply the biographical context of Plato's work, interesting though that is. A small and neat summary of Plato's life is given in R.M. Hare, *Plato* (Oxford: Oxford University Press, 1982, Past Masters series), pp. 1–8.

6. Socrates left no writings. His execution, on conviction for the corruption of youth (i.e. spreading dissension, rather than any more lurid crime), appalled Plato, and many of the early works are defences of and justifications for Socrates' philosophical method.

7. It is standard academic practice to refer to passages in Plato via the numbering of the early edition by Stephanus. These are given in the margin of most editions of Plato's works.

8. For a discussion of the interpretative difficulties, see Robin Waterfield's essay in his edition of the *Theaetetus* (Harmondsworth: Penguin, 1987), pp. 218–25, which includes the classic references.

9. For an interesting discussion of this ancient prejudice against writing see Jorge Luis Borges, 'On the Cult of Books', in *The Total Library: Non-Fiction 1922–1986*, ed. Eliot Weinberger, trans. Esther Allen and Suzanne Jill Levine (London: Penguin, 2000), pp. 358–62.

10. A.J. Ayer, *The Problem of Knowledge* (Harmondsworth: Penguin, 1956), pp. 7–35.

11. Susan Haack, *Evidence and Inquiry: Towards Reconstruction in Epistemology* (Oxford: Blackwell, 1993).

12. Fred I. Dretske, *Knowledge and the Flow of Information* (Oxford: Blackwell, 1981), pp. 85–106.

13. Timothy Williamson, *Knowledge and its Limits* (Oxford: Clarendon Press, 2000).

14. Ludwig Wittgenstein, *On Certainty* (Oxford: Blackwell, 1969), ed. Gertrude E.M. Anscombe, G.H. von Wright and Denis Paul.

15. Nicholas Everitt and Alec Fisher, *Modern Epistemology: A New Introduction* (New York: McGraw-Hill, 1995), pp. 17–50.

16. Ibid., pp. 48–9.

17. This is not, perhaps, a major moment in intellectual history, but for the record the paper in question is: Kieron O'Hara, 'Sceptical Overkill: On Two Recent Arguments Against Scepticism', *Mind*, vol. 102 (1993), pp. 315–27. For Descartes, see the *Meditations on First Philosophy*, particularly the first meditation, which is in a number of editions, including John Cottingham, Robert Stoothoff and Dugald Murdoch (eds.), *The Philosophical Writings of Descartes: Volume II* (Cambridge: Cambridge University Press, 1985), pp. 1–62.

18. Lyotard, op. cit., p. 4.

19. Most of the figures in this section have been taken from Varian's heroic – and entertaining – study, available at http://www.sims.berkeley.edu/research/projects/how-much-info/summary.html.

20. Statistic from Matthew Symonds, 'Haves and Have Nots', in 'Government and the Internet' survey, *The*

Economist (24 June 2000), pp. 19–23.

21. For a dismissive account of the Internet, see Gordon Graham, *The Internet: A Philosophical Inquiry* (London: Routledge, 1999). I have criticised this book in a review (written with Louise Crow) in *International Studies in the Philosophy of Science*, vol. 15 (2001), and in an article on 'Democracy and the Internet', in the Web journal *Ends and Means*, at http://www.abdn.ac.uk/philosophy/cpts/ohara.hti. For a worry about the effects on democracy and free speech, see Cass Sunstein, *Republic.com* (Princeton: Princeton University Press, 2001). The classic account of the effect of printing on Western civilisation is Marshall McLuhan, *The Gutenberg Galaxy* (Toronto: University of Toronto Press, 1962).

22. Lyotard, op. cit., p. 4.

23. Examples of important and interesting works on organisations include Kenneth J. Arrow, *The Limits of Organization* (New York: Norton, 1974) and Mary Douglas, *How Institutions Think* (London: Routledge, 1987). Charles Jonscher writes very well about the importance of retaining the human element in such discussions in *Wiredlife: Who Are We in the Digital Age?* (London: Anchor, 1999).

24. 'The China Syndrome', *The Economist* (25 August 2001), p. 33.

25. Longer discussions of these six challenges can be found at the AKT Website at http://www.aktors.org.

26. The Gettier experiments appear in Edmund Gettier,

'Is Justified True Belief Knowledge?', *Analysis*, vol. 23 (1963), pp. 121–3. This paper is reprinted in a couple of more accessible collections of philosophical essays, and Everitt and Fisher discuss the arguments in *Modern Epistemology*, op. cit., pp. 21–9.

27. Raymond Reiter, 'A Logic for Default Reasoning', *Artificial Intelligence*, vol. 13 (1980), pp. 81–132.

Further Reading

A good general survey of and introduction to epistemo-
logy is Nicholas Everitt and Alec Fisher, *Modern
Epistemology: A New Introduction* (New York:
McGraw-Hill, 1995).

In this book I have touched upon only a few of the
issues raised by Plato's philosophy. Dave Robinson
and Judy Groves, *Introducing Plato* (Cambridge: Icon
Books, 2000), gives a general overview of his work
and influence. One of the many virtues of Plato is that
he is one of the few philosophers who can be read for
pleasure. To read Plato's epistemological works, start
with W. K. C. Guthrie (trans.), *Protagoras and Meno*
(London: Penguin, 1956). Both are useful, but the
Meno is particularly important. More difficult, but
central to understanding Plato's epistemology, is the
Theaetetus: see Robin Waterfield (trans.), *Theaetetus*
(London: Penguin, 1987), or Myles Burnyeat (ed.),
The Theaetetus of Plato (Indianapolis: Hackett,
1990), which contains the text translated by M. J.
Levett. The important book-length essays by Water-
field and Burnyeat are invaluable for the student of
Plato, and give a good guide to the issues and the liter-
ature. Another useful early piece is Walter Hamilton
(trans.), *Gorgias* (London: Penguin, 1960).

The history and general pattern of scepticism is given in the essays in Myles Burnyeat (ed.), *The Skeptical Tradition* (Berkeley: University of California Press, 1983).

A nice little reference book for the Internet is John Cowpertwait and Simon Flynn, *The Internet from A to Z* (Cambridge: Icon Books, 2001). I particularly like the appendix on emoticons or smileys. An altogether heftier tome is Margaret Levine Young, Doug Muder, Dave Kay, Kathy Warfel and Alison Burrows, *Internet: Millenium Edition: The Complete Reference* (Berkeley: Osborne McGraw-Hill, 1999, but regularly updated).

Charles Jonscher, *Wiredlife: Who Are We in the Digital Age?* (London: Anchor, 1999), is an excellent history of information technology, with an important focus on the human element.

The knowledge economy, and the way it rewards creativity, is discussed in John Howkins, *The Creative Economy: How People Make Money From Ideas* (London: Penguin, 2001).

A perceptive analysis, or prediction, of the effect of technology on knowledge is in the classic Jean-François Lyotard, *The Postmodern Condition: A Report on Knowledge,* translated by Geoff

Bennington and Brian Massumi, with a foreword by Fredric Jameson (Manchester: Manchester University Press, 1984).

The World Wide Web Consortium (W3C) administers HTML; its website is at http://www.w3c.org. A brief, clear statement of the importance of XML can be found in Tim Berners-Lee, James Hendler and Ora Lassila, 'The Semantic Web', *Scientific American*, May 2001, available at http://www.scientificamerican .com/2001/0501issue/0501berners-lee.html. The manifesto of the AKT project is available at http://www. aktors.org/publications/Manifesto.doc.

Perhaps the most influential book on knowledge management of late is Ikujiro Nonaka and Hirotaka Takeuchi, *The Knowledge-Creating Company: How Japanese Companies Create the Dynamics of Innovation* (Oxford: Oxford University Press, 1995).

Key Ideas

Data are collections of symbols.

Epistemology is the philosophical study of know-ledge. It addresses questions such as: what knowledge is; what kinds of knowledge there are; where know-ledge comes from; whether there are things that we can't know; how we can know what we don't know, and look for it. Clearly such issues are strongly related, for example, to the study of science and how science progresses. A great deal of epistemological research has been aimed at confounding *scepticism*. Plato was the first epistemologist of any note; a list of greats would include Aristotle, Descartes, Spinoza, Leibniz, Locke, Berkeley, Hume, Kant, J.S. Mill, Bertrand Russell and W.V.O. Quine. Important writers who have made contributions working currently include Donald Davidson, Alvin Goldman, Susan Haack, Jürgen Habermas, Robert Nozick, Richard Rorty and Timothy Williamson.

Information is understandable *data*, data with a meaning.

Information overload is the situation, common in modern society, where someone has everything he or she needs to perform a task, but it is buried in a pile of irrelevant information; the person then may not have the time or resources to find the important stuff. Hence possession of the information is not sufficient for it to be of any use.

The **Internet** is the technological advance that has allowed anyone who can get onto the telephone network and has a suitable receiving system (e.g., a computer, a mobile phone) to access any of billions of computer data files. The relevant technologies are very simple: TCP/IP and dynamic routing. The net effect – no pun intended – is to bring the largest quantity of information ever gathered together within everyone's reach.

Know-how is a type of knowledge often ignored by epistemologists, yet is (a) a very common type of knowledge, and (b) extremely important as far as the knowledge economy goes. Representing know-how, rather than propositional knowledge, is one of the most imperative tasks of the version of *epistemology* outlined in this book. In the knowledge-management literature, the terms used for know-how and propositional knowledge are *procedural knowledge* and *declarative knowledge* respectively.

Knowledge is a type of *information* that aids the performance of effective actions. Traditionally, *epistemologists* have focused on the psychological aspects of knowledge; however, modern conditions – the *knowledge economy* – have shown the need to expand the definition of knowledge to include non-psychological states.

Knowledge acquisition is the process of adding knowledge to an agent's stock (the agent can be human, or non-human such as an organisation). Tasks for a reconstructed *epistemology* include: outlining reliable methods for acquiring knowledge from people, computers and economic markets; and finding ways of discovering knowledge that exists only implicitly within an organisation and making it explicit.

The **knowledge economy** is one in which knowledge is a force of production and a source of competitive advantage. The exploitation of raw materials and labour characterised the so-called old economy; the knowledge economy involves a general switch to services from manufacturing, and places a premium on an educated and productive workforce.

Knowledge management is the task of making sure that an organisation's consumption, acquisition and use of knowledge is cost-effective. In other words, the task of: ensuring that any knowledge that the organisation possesses is used as often and efficiently as possible; ensuring that any knowledge that the organisation needs but does not possess is acquired; ensuring that all the knowledge the organisation possesses adds as much as possible to the organisation's effectiveness.

Knowledge sharing is a tricky part of *knowledge management*. Within an organisation, particularly a big or widely spread one, it is often the case that the knowledge that organisation possesses does not get to the people who need it. Employee X does not know that employee Y knows how to solve X's current problem. The aim of knowledge sharing is to ensure that X can find out who in the organisation can help him or her, without contributing too much to *information overload*.

Scepticism is a type of philosophical objection to a theory, objecting to the basic assumptions of that theory. Sceptical arguments are usually very pernicious, and the net result of *epistemological* scepticism has been that, over the millennia, epistemologists have spent much too much effort trying to confound the sceptic and not enough finding out about knowledge, and therefore modern-day epistemology is not adequate for the serious epistemological problems of knowledge management and the knowledge economy.

The **Semantic Web** is a development of the *World Wide Web*, involving the use of the markup language XML which allows a Webpage to include within it a specification of the knowledge it contains. This will allow much more intelligent searching and navigation of the Web.

The **World Wide Web** is a portion of the *Internet* which provides a common format for multimedia computer files to be displayed on-screen through a browser. It exploits the markup language HTML, which governs the display of data on-screen, and is not tied to any one operating system (such as Windows or Linux). This gives the Web a common look and feel, wherever you are accessing it from.

In case of difficulty in obtaining any Icon title through normal channels, books can be purchased through BOOKPOST.
Tel: + 44 1624 836000 Fax: + 44 1624 837033
E-mail: bookshop@enterprise.net
www.bookpost.co.uk

Please quote 'Ref: Faber' when placing your order.

If you require further assistance, please contact:
info@iconbooks.co.uk

Other titles in the *Postmodern Encounters* series: